A Storm of Horses
The Story of Artist Rosa Bonheur

Written and Illustrated by

Ruth Sanderson

Crocodile Books, USA

An imprint of Interlink Publishing Group, Inc.

www.interlinkbooks.com

First published 2022 by

CROCODILE BOOKS
An imprint of Interlink Publishing Group, Inc.
46 Crosby Street, Northampton, MA 01060
www.interlinkbooks.com

Library of Congress Cataloging-in-Publication data available
ISBN-13: 978-1-62371-848-0

The illustrations for this book were created in oils on Giverny paper
Rosa Bonheur's name is pronounced roh-zah bohn-uhr

Printed and bound in Korea

This book is dedicated to Katherine Brault

She and her family are tirelessly working to preserve Rosa Bonheur's home, studio, artwork, and gardens, at the Château de Rosa Bonheur in Thomery, France, and to raise public awareness for the life and work of this phenomenal 19th century woman artist.

Rosa Bonheur galloped into the world in 1822, the year of her birth in France, and never stopped.

Rosa's father Raymond was an artist. He painted her portrait when she was four years old, clutching a toy in one hand and a pencil in the other. Rosa wanted to be an artist too.

Rosa loved playing "knights," with her brother Isodore as the horse. She used a cord as reins, a paintbrush for a bit, and a big stick as her sword. A few years later at boarding school, her father took her to a special ceremony where she was made an honorary Knight Templar and gifted a wooden sword.

Rosa felt like a woman-warrior.

One night at school she noticed mysterious shadows outside her bedroom window. Rosa grabbed her sword. Soon the enemy knights were vanquished! The next day the headmistress discovered her prize flowers lying on the ground, and sent Rosa trotting back home. Rosa was delighted. She'd been bored at school and covered her papers with animal sketches and funny drawings of the teachers.

Rosa's father sat her down in his own art studio in Paris with pencils, paper and clay, and plaster casts of animals. Finally Rosa could sketch and sculpt as much as she wanted.

In those days people expected women to get married and have children. They did not usually have careers or support themselves. Rosa had no interest in ever getting married. She loved horses and other animals and wanted to learn to draw and paint them. Just as she'd steered her brother in horse play, she began to steer her life toward that purpose, and never stopped.

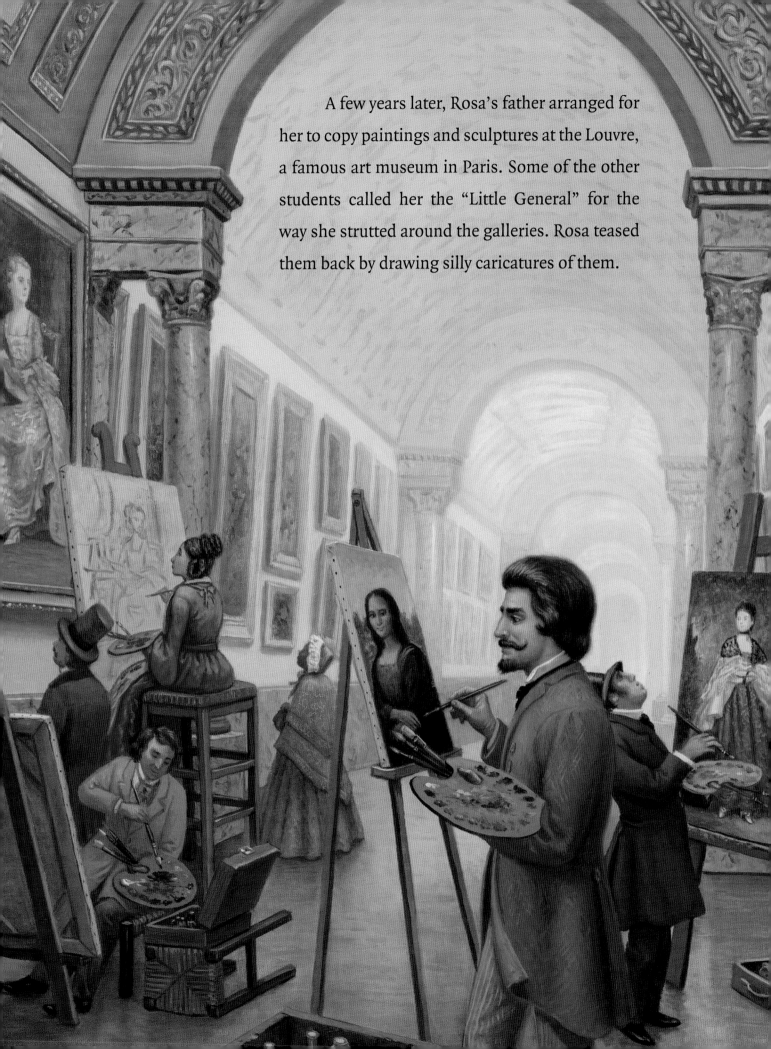

A few years later, Rosa's father arranged for her to copy paintings and sculptures at the Louvre, a famous art museum in Paris. Some of the other students called her the "Little General" for the way she strutted around the galleries. Rosa teased them back by drawing silly caricatures of them.

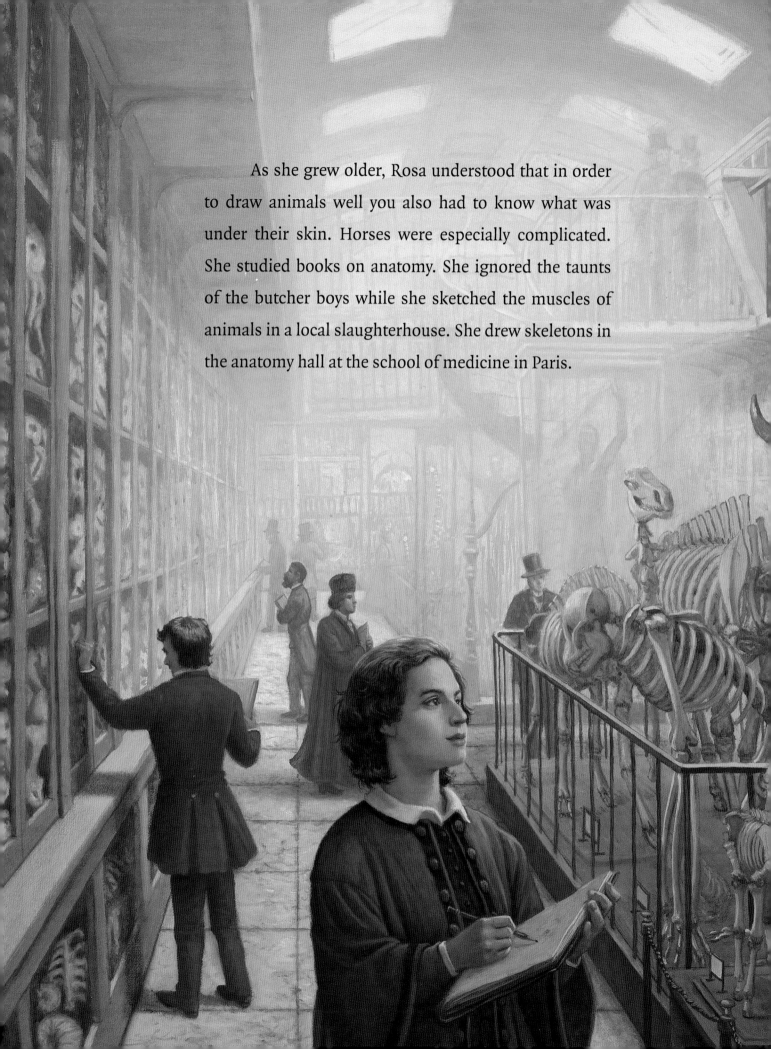

As she grew older, Rosa understood that in order to draw animals well you also had to know what was under their skin. Horses were especially complicated. She studied books on anatomy. She ignored the taunts of the butcher boys while she sketched the muscles of animals in a local slaughterhouse. She drew skeletons in the anatomy hall at the school of medicine in Paris.

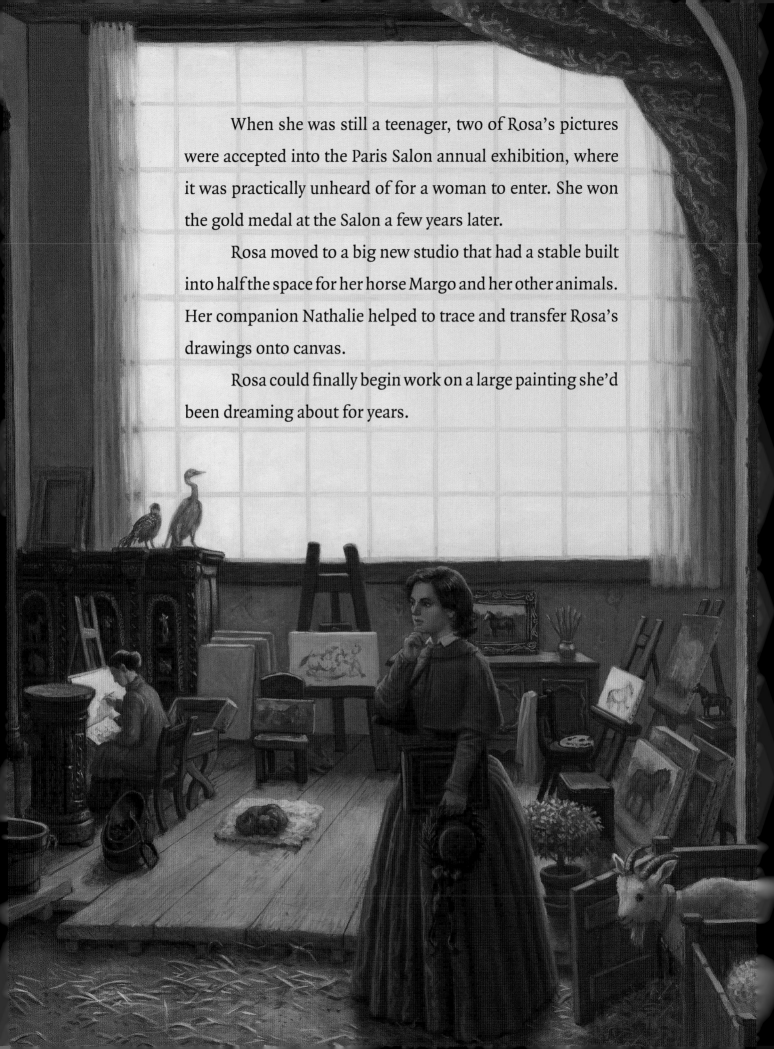

When she was still a teenager, two of Rosa's pictures were accepted into the Paris Salon annual exhibition, where it was practically unheard of for a woman to enter. She won the gold medal at the Salon a few years later.

Rosa moved to a big new studio that had a stable built into half the space for her horse Margo and her other animals. Her companion Nathalie helped to trace and transfer Rosa's drawings onto canvas.

Rosa could finally begin work on a large painting she'd been dreaming about for years.

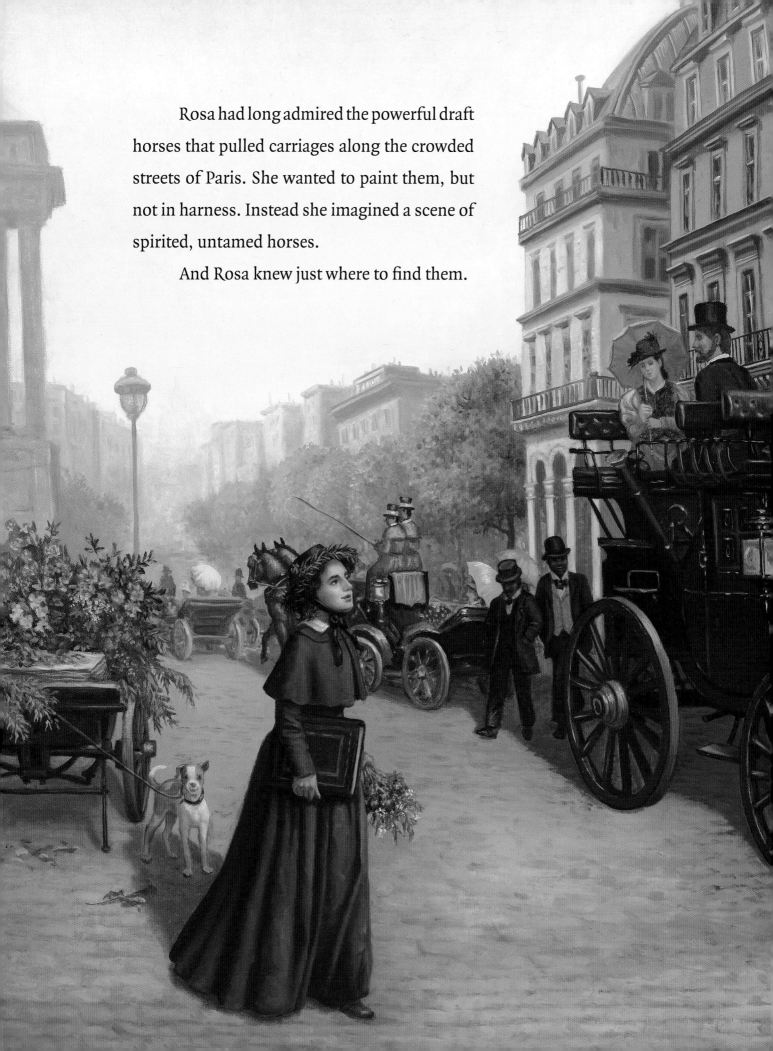

Rosa had long admired the powerful draft horses that pulled carriages along the crowded streets of Paris. She wanted to paint them, but not in harness. Instead she imagined a scene of spirited, untamed horses.

And Rosa knew just where to find them.

Twice a week men bought and sold horses in Paris at a horse market. There was one problem. Women were not allowed. The crowded market was considered too dangerous for women in their long skirts, and it was illegal for women to wear pants in those days.

That did not stop Rosa! She approached the police, and they granted her a permit to dress in men's clothes so she could attend without being noticed.

Rosa was pleased with her disguise. For the next year and a half Rosa filled her sketchbooks with drawings of the horses and their handlers.

She drew powerful Percherons prancing in circles for potential buyers.

She drew horses with feet flying,
eyes wide, and nostrils flaring.

Rosa drew a storm of horses.

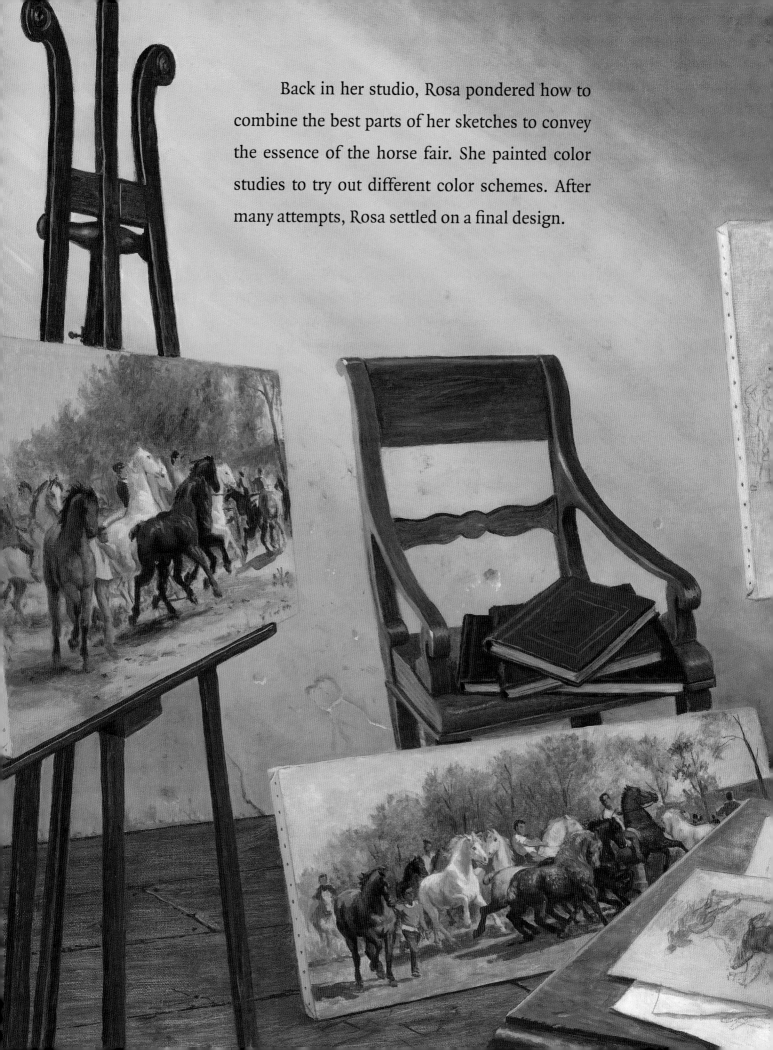

Back in her studio, Rosa pondered how to combine the best parts of her sketches to convey the essence of the horse fair. She painted color studies to try out different color schemes. After many attempts, Rosa settled on a final design.

Rosa was ready to begin the largest and most challenging painting of her life on a canvas eight feet tall by sixteen and a half feet wide.

After transferring her design, Rosa drew out the basic outlines with burnt red ochre oil paint. She rubbed the background with a neutral gray. When that dried, she began to add layers of color, climbing a ladder to reach the top part of the picture.

Rosa spent the next year expressing her love of horses in oil paint on canvas.

At the Paris Salon exhibition in 1853, no one could believe that a woman created this painting of horses so full of energy and movement. People thought women could only paint much tamer subjects. But Rosa had her own ideas.

The painting called *The Horse Fair* is Rosa Bonheur's masterpiece. It portrays both the form and the spirit of horses in a beautiful realistic rendering. Viewers standing in front of this painting feel a sense of wonder that these magnificent beasts allow themselves to be tamed at all.

The Horse Fair, 1853-55. The Metropolitan Museum of Art, New York.

Like the horses she loved, Rosa was spirited too, and untamed by society's expectations. She proved that a woman artist could achieve success in a time when men dominated both the art world and all aspects of public life.

Rosa simply charged ahead.

MORE ABOUT ROSA

Rosa's birth name was Marie-Rosalie Bonheur. Sadly, her mother Sophie died when Rosa was just eleven years old. Because her mother had always called her Rosa, she decided to use that name for the signature on her art, in remembrance of the love she had for her departed parent.

Rosa was an *animalier*, a term used in the nineteenth century for artists who specialized in realistic paintings of animals. These kinds of lifelike, detailed paintings were very popular during Rosa's lifetime, and she was able to support herself and her family by selling her artwork. Besides horses, Rosa painted scenes with bulls, sheep, oxen, goats, and other animals. She said that "nature was my teacher," and spent a great deal of time at local farms, drawing all the various animals. "I really got into studying their ways, especially the expressions in their eyes. Isn't the eye the mirror of the soul for each and every living creature?"

Women were not allowed to attend art schools with men in those days. It was through Rosa's own dedicated effort that she was able to master her skills—by studying anatomy books, going to local slaughterhouses, drawing animal skeletons, copying paintings, learning from her father, and sketching live animals. Birds, sheep, goats, ducks, rabbits, quail, a pet squirrel, and even a few rats, flew or frolicked freely about the studio. Her first painting accepted at the Paris Salon exhibition depicted two rabbits eating carrots. When she was older, Rosa made sketching trips to the Pyrenees, Auvergne, Scotland, and Birmingham, and created paintings inspired by her studies of animals there.

Edouard Louis Dubufe painted Rosa's portrait in 1857, just a few years after her success with *The Horse Fair*. Rosa found the portrait dull, and asked the artist's permission to paint a bull into the picture instead of the table he originally painted. As a result, the buyer paid both Dubufe and Rosa for their separate parts of the painting!

Rosa chose to never marry. Instead, she lived with a beloved lifelong partner, Nathalie Micas. Nathalie dedicated her life to making it possible for Rosa to concentrate on her painting and not worry about daily household matters. In addition to tracing and transferring some of

Rosa's sketches to canvases, Nathalie also worked on some of her paintings, as did Rosa's brothers and sister. This was a common practice in those times.

Nathalie died in 1889. That year Rosa met a talented young American painter, Anna Klumpke, who was visiting Paris. Anna eventually traveled back to France a number of years later to paint Rosa's portrait. The two artists became very close and Anna remained at Rosa's château until Rosa's death in 1899.

Many believe that Rosa was a lesbian, though she never spoke publicly about her preferences. In the biography Anna Klumpke wrote that was published after Rosa's death, she quotes Rosa talking about her feelings for Nathalie: "If I had been a man, I would have married her, and nobody would have dreamed up those silly stories." And when Anna agreed to live with her until the artist's "last breath," Rosa said, "This will be the divine marriage of two souls…" Rosa defied tradition in bequeathing her entire estate to Anna, when it otherwise would have gone to her brother, a male relative. This indicated a bond as strong as a licensed marriage, impossible for two women in those times. Because of Anna, Rosa's home and much of her work was preserved.

Rosa's painting *The Horse Fair* (*Le Marché aux Chevaux* in original French) was greeted with great enthusiasm at the Paris Salon in 1853, by both critics and the public, and it created quite a sensation. Rosa's agent Ernest Gambart of London then arranged for the original painting to tour Great Britain's major cities. Queen Victoria and Prince Albert admired the painting greatly in a private viewing at Buckingham Palace. Critics praised the painting as work of genius, and huge crowds paid to see it. Rosa created a smaller version of the painting for the National Gallery in London so that artist Thomas Landseer could more easily copy it to make an engraved print version.

The Horse Fair was sold to an American collector in 1857. With all the publicity she had received for the painting, Rosa became a star, and her fame and fortune continued to rise for the rest of her life. Her paintings were sought after by collectors. A Rosa Bonheur doll was even produced!

After her success with *The Horse Fair*, Rosa was able to purchase a house called the Château de By in Thomery, near the forest of Fontainebleau. She continued to dress in masculine clothes for the rest of her life, although she still wore dresses to formal public events. Over the years she kept a menagerie of animals there, as both pets and models, including horses, dogs, an otter, a stag, a gazelle, wild boars, monkeys, cages of birds, and even a few lions!

Empress Eugénie, the wife of Louis-Napoleon Bonaparte, visited her at By and was quite impressed with Rosa and her work. In 1865, the empress bestowed the Grand Cross of the French Legion of Honor on Rosa. Her arrival was a surprise, and Rosa had barely enough time to change out of her pants and painting smock and into a dress to receive her royal guest.

When William "Buffalo Bill" Cody brought his Wild West Show to Paris in 1889 Rosa became fascinated with the stories and legends of the American West. She sketched and painted the cowboys and Indigenous Americans who worked in the show. She painted a portrait of Cody mounted on his favorite gray horse. Rosa painted many more scenes of the Wild West, which sold especially well in the United States.

After changing hands a few times, *The Horse Fair* was purchased by Cornelius Vanderbilt in 1887. He immediately donated the painting to the Metropolitan Museum of Art in New York City, where it is still hanging today in all its glory.

Rosa's realistic style of painting fell into disfavor after her death with the rise of Impressionism and the Modern Art era. For much of the twentieth century, paintings by artists working in traditional realistic styles were dismisssed by critics as outdated and lacking in innovation.

This, along with the fact that she was a woman, caused her work to be largely forgotten by critics and the public. In recent years, along with that of other historic and important women artists, Rosa's work has begun to receive due recognition for its excellence and its rightful place in the continuum of art history.

Open to the public for tours, the Château de Rosa Bonheur in Thomery, France, is preserved and presented much as it would have appeared during the forty years Rosa lived and worked there.

AUTHOR'S NOTE

Almost fifty years ago I stood awestruck in front of a gigantic painting of horses at the Metropolitan Museum of Art in New York City. *The Horse Fair* by Rosa Bonheur impressed me with its detailed realism, dramatic lighting, and its energy and sense of movement. It remains my favorite horse painting to this day. Another one of Rosa's paintings gave me the idea for this book.

A few years ago I came across her unfinished painting of horses on the internet, shown above. I learned it was on display at the Château de Rosa Bonheur. This picture gave me the idea to write and illustrate a story that focused on Rosa's process of creating *The Horse Fair*, since I could directly see the way she handled the stages of a painting of horses. In my research I was thrilled to learn many more details about her painting process and her remarkable life. And when I was able to visit her preserved home and studio in 2019, I was moved to tears to see her work in person.

Like Rosa, my love of horses and learning to draw them were my main inspiration for becoming an artist. When I was a teenager my first oil painting was a portrait of a horse. I decided at the Paier School of Art that I wanted to learn to paint realistically. I also wanted to create pictures that told a story, like illustrators Arthur Rackham, Norman Rockwell, N.C. Wyeth, and women artists like Beatrix Potter, Kate Greenaway, and Jessie Willcox Smith. I was happy to find a home in children's book illustration after art school, and I've illustrated many horse stories in my long career, including my fairy tale retelling, *The Golden Mare, the Firebird, and the Magic Ring*.

Rosa describes her goal for another large horse painting, *Threshing Wheat*, and this quote might easily apply to *The Horse Fair* as well: "It is my dream to show horses snorting fire and dust welling up around their hooves. I want this infernal waltz, this wild tornado to make people's head's spin." With *The Horse Fair*, Rosa certainly realized this dream.

My dream is to shine a light on this little-known woman artist, who was born two hundred years ago and yet accomplished so much in a time when men dominated the art world.

And, of course I hope to inspire other horse-loving young artists.

RECOMMENDED DRAWING BOOKS

Drawing Horses by Ruth Sanderson

How to Draw Horses by Walter Foster

How to Draw Animals by Jack Hamm

Draw Horses with Sam Savitt

Draw 50 Horses by Lee J. Ames

SOURCES

Ashton, Dore and Denise Browne Hare. *Rosa Bonheur, A Life and Legend*. Viking Press, 1981.

Hallon, John Stephen. *Paris Salon Exhibitions 1667–1880*. Pacific Lutheran University. https://sites.google.com/a/plu.edu/paris-salon-exhibitions-1667-1880.

Klumpke, Anna. *Rosa Bonheur : The Artist's (Auto)biography*. Translated by Gretchen van Slyke. Ann Arbor: The University of Michigan Press, 1997.

Stanton, Theodore. *The Reminiscences of Rosa Bonheur*. London: Andrew Melrose, 1920.

Shriver, Rosalia. *Rosa Bonheur: With a Checklist of Works in American Collections*. New Jersey: Associated University Presses, 1982.

Texier, Edmund. *Tableau de Paris*, Paris, 1849.

Weisberg, Gabriel P. , et al. *Rosa Bonheur: All Nature's Children*. New York: Dahesh Museum, 1998.

IMAGE CREDITS

(All paintings are by Rosa Bonheur unless otherwise noted)

p. 32-33: *The Horse Fair*, 1853-55. The Metropolitan Museum of Art, New York, United States. Gift of Cornelius Vanderbilt, 1887. www.metmuseum.org.

p. 34: *Ploughing in the Nivernais*, 1849. Musée d'Orsay, France.

p. 35: *Rosa Bonheur*, 1857, by Louis Dubufe. Palace of Versailles, France

p. 36: *The Lion at Home*, 1881. Ferens Art Gallery, Hull Museums, United Kingdom.

p. 37: *Buffalo Bill Cody*, 1889. Whitney Gallery of Western Art, Wyoming, United States.

p. 37: *Château de Rosa Bonheur*, 2019. Photo by Ruth Sanderson.

p. 38: *Race of Wild Horses*, detail of unfinished painting. Château de Rosa Bonheur.

WHERE TO SEE MORE WORK BY ROSA BONHEUR

UNITED STATES

Brooklyn Museum, New York

Art Institute of Chicago, Illinois

Dahesh Museum of Art, New York

Cleveland Museum of Art, Ohio

Fine Art Museums of San Francisco, California

Haggin Museum, California

Harvard Art Museums, Massachusetts

Metropolitan Museum of Art, New York

Minneapolis Institute of Arts, Minnesota

National Museum of Women in the Arts, Washington, D.C.

Ringling Museum of Art, Florida

Whitney Western Art Museum, Wyoming

FRANCE AND OTHER COUNTRIES

Art Gallery of Ontario, Canada

Bilbao Fine Arts Museum, Spain

Château de Fontainebleau, France

Ferens Art Gallery, Hull Museums, UK

Musée des Beaux-Arts de Bordeaux, France

Musée du Louvre, Paris, France

National Gallery, London, UK

Musée d'Orsay, Paris, France

Château de Rosa Bonheur, Thomery, France